FROM THE BLOCK TO THE BOARDROOM

WILLIAM JACKSON

WRITERS REPUBLIC L.L.C.
515 Summit Ave. Unit R1
Union City, NJ 07087, USA

Website: *www.writersrepublic.com*
Hotline: *1-877-656-6838*
Email: *info@writersrepublic.com*

Ordering Information:
Quantity sales. Special discounts are available on quantity purchases by corporations, associations, and others. For details, contact the publisher at the address above.

Library of Congress Control Number: 2020937921
ISBN-13:   978-1-64620-350-5   [Paperback Edition]
                  978-1-64620-351-2   [Digital Edition]

Rev. date: 05/19/2020

INTRO

I've recently learned that life is a constant process of bettering yourself. And that you as a person must do all in your power to continue to do so until you no longer exist. So, the concept for this book came when I was about two weeks from being released. I had just completed a five-year seven-month sentence. During that time, I feel like every part of me was tested from my character, to my soul down to my mental capacity. In some strange way I feel like the time I spent being incarcerated saved my life in some way. I really thank God everyday for helping me out of that situation. And that he placed positive individuals in my life that keep me from self-sabotage. Self- sabotage is anytime you prevent yourself from doing something good or positive by doing something foolish or idiotic. These moments can happen in the drop of a dime under certain situations. That was seven years ago. I believe in the beginning this book coming together was just a wet dream. Something to the effect of yeah if I write this book, I could change my family's life somehow. So, I thought a little bit more on the subject, still being idol doing nothing in terms of getting my dreams out. So, then my thought was that maybe something may happen or if I actually try. Then boom!! Truth being told it didn't even happen like that. Honestly, through a lot of ups and downs this narrative was put together. With hopes of giving the next person an easier journey in this triathlon of life.

To be honest I don't believe that I was able to compose this in 2012 nor was I ready to do so. I didn't have the knowledge or the will just yet. I still had faith that one day I would be able to put this together and give it to the masses in hopes that one person relates and tries to do something different with their lives. Throughout those seven years I believe I have seen the best and worst characteristics in human beings and what society has to offer a person with the same demographic characteristics. But that isn't necessarily a good or bad thing. You can learn a lot from anyone you just have to take the time to figure out what's going on and what is the ultimate goal that you would like to obtain.

1. A person's ability to teach. Some people instruct or give directions. They don't teach a person what they are trying to learn or break down into steps how to achieve the concept. A teacher will show you how to achieve the best solution for whatever kind of problem. For example, a math teacher cannot simply say give me the answer to this equation, no they have to break down the problem in a step by step logical sequential order. Once this is complete then the correct answer should be shown. But if not, the teacher can go back step by step and show each process and explain how not to make mistakes while getting there.

2. A person's ability to transition. Everyone doesn't transition well. Some people have been stuck doing the same routine for several years. Even with knowing the results are not positive at all people still wallow in their own madness. I was told as a child that the definition of insanity is committing the same acts numerous times and thinking the results will just change somehow on their own without any assistance. I am here to tell you that nothing will change for the better easily and without a fight. Especially if it is a habit or something that we as humans have done for a while or they are accustomed to seeing others do so.

3. The hardest thing about life is that it is constantly evolving. Nothing is the same as it was yesterday. We must also change to better succeed at life. Jobs are more demanding of the employee and the competitiveness of the workforce will only increase as time goes on. With that being said the only option is to follow your dreams and to gain all the know how to accomplish these dreams.

   Knowledge. After something is learned for the most part the only way to demonstrate the mastering of said skill or ability is to teach it. Show someone that has no idea or is waiting for luck to turn their way. At some point in life you may have to make your own luck. I remember in the age of compact discs, after a recent purchase I would find myself reading the pamphlet that would be on the inside. There was valuable information in that reading that many people didn't pay attention to at all. Some artist would put a little message or tell a story as to why they wrote a song and their mindset while composing. Those feelings of joy, pain, happiness or sorrow are used to create something positive. I hope after reading this short story the reader can do the same. And scale or size or deed doesn't matter as long as the actions come from the heart. I try to do positive things that will benefit me and secondly my family. As a man I must provide etcetera etcetera. Well in turn this benefits the community. Then boom our respective communities are a bit better the stereotypes that plague our communities no longer are the narrative they are a misconception.

No journey is possible without faith and hope. Faith is complete trust or confidence in something. In this case faith is knowing that there is a better way to provide for yourself and your family. Hope is the thought and preparation it takes you to get there. From the block to the boardroom is a transition that takes time, hard work and perseverance. Which would in turn develop into a work ethic. Work ethic is the belief that hard work and diligence have a moral benefit to the worker and to that person's coworkers. It gives the person an ability a strength or value that builds character and self-esteem. It is a set of values centered on the importance of efficient and effective work being done and manifested by determination or the desire to work hard. My only problem with working hard is that sometimes in a workplace your hard work may lead to less work being done by others. During my personal journey from my block to the boardroom I have had plenty of jobs. For one reason or another I managed to separate myself from these employers. I personally had to learn that failure is a part of success. The main point is to keep trying after said failure which is really a lesson. I hope that after reading this the reader is better equipped with tools that will further their success.

THE BLOCK

I'm sure many of you have seen the uplifting quotes on social media referring to if you can lead a gang you can run a company. Well I am here to say that the quote has some validity to it. So, the block is a place where young black men use to conjugate. Now I say the block, but this can be a neighborhood hangout. When I was a kid, I'd see family members hanging out and being social. So, there is a difference from being on the porch and being off it. While being on the porch you may see the ups and the downs of those individuals involved with the streets. Honestly this should be a warning a strong visual as to what may happen if this line of work is chosen. More often than none it's what draws the younger generation into a whole new world without understanding the consequences of their actions. Which leads to further destruction, but I'll get to that later. Certain things are being glorified in the media and in music and movies that portrays "hustling" or "trapping" as something of civil rights proportions. That which it is not. I can recall a conversation I had with a friend of mine some years back and he said, "How can I tell the younger generation what to or not to do?" I didn't know what to say to that, so I merely just listened. Today I would say that no matter if I have a job to give someone, I'll tell them they need one. Whether you hopped in feet first or didn't have a choice the end results for many who attempt are jail or death.

Proper Planning Prevents Poor Performance. Different situations I've been fortunate to make it out of have framed my mind a certain way and rightfully so. I thank God for those situations. Hopefully it will make things smoother. For example, when a lion is in his natural habitat, he lives his life as regularly scheduled. One day he may have the unfortunate experience of being placed in a zoo. He may never have a problem until one day his animal instincts takeover. And then the true essence of this beast is known. Human beings are creatures of habit. Meaning that once we know or think we know a situation we know how to attack it. This is not necessarily true, and I feel this is where we make our 1St mistakes. Nothing in life stays the same. Everything is constantly changing evolving and we must do the same. If not, we risk being overlapped or overwhelmed. Being overlapped is just like what happens during a track race. Not handling your business and possibly being more concerned with what someone else is doing could be devastating to you and those around you. As promised earlier sometimes the environment we are in can capture us and engulf us in it. In this case the block can turn into a cell or prison bunk very fast. I would be doing everyone a great disservice if I omitted that. If this ever happens count your blessing because it could be a wake-up call and receive it as such.

While I was incarcerated, I worked on myself and wrote down feasible goals to be obtained once I was released. Again, if ever faced with that reality focus on the positive and overcome it. I kept busy for the most part and even worked for .45$ an hour. That itself was a miracle as well as humbling. Finally, the powers that be take advantage of those who's mentality may be weaker than the ones before them. And in this instance an individual may say something or do something that goes against what any respectful man should do. To cooperate with law enforcement is a very negative aspect of block life. To become an informant and do the work for these individuals is kind of like selling your soul. Any of those situations further damage the community as well as tarnish the individuals and their family members reputation forever. By accepting the fact that an error has been made and taking responsibility for your actions will allow the healing process to start. The block will give you all the worldly possessions you want or desire. These worldly possessions can disappear faster than they were collected. Leaving you paralyzed both physically and mentally with what occurred so quickly and within a blink of the eye. There comes a point when even at your best you envision something greater than your current situation. All the older gentleman I saw searched for a way out. Whether it's a business or property management they took that step to do better, to be better than their current situation. And that's what most of us aspire to do in life. The goal in any business transaction is to walk away satisfied. Whether the customer or the supplier you want to be pleased with what just happened. As the seller you want to do business that leads your customers to want to continually do more business with you. As a customer the role is reversed. You have to still present yourself as a businessperson and have some sort of dignity with what you present to the public. Business is business. It doesn't matter if the act takes place in a back ally in Detroit. Or if it happens in a skyscraper in New York City. What matters is the way that the business is conducted. We are in the finesse age. Everyone wants what they want, and they want it right now. The only problem with that is that haste makes waste. Some people will pray on your emotions and in this case your anxiousness. This can be disastrous. To prevent that I'd go with something I was told as a child. If it sounds too good to be true nine times out of ten it is probably a scam.

YOUR SUPPORT SYSTEM

Well unfortunately everyone won't have the same external support system. The good news it all starts with you. It doesn't matter who does or does not support you. Support yourself to the fullest. Create your own support system. This can include family members, friends and associates. There is a saying about people you've known since elementary school Day 1's. Well I am here to tell you that all Day 1's will not be going to be there for Day 2. However, meeting new positive individuals that share the same mindset will make achievements a bit easier. Besides that, have a plan for yourself. To write down a list of goals that will improve your lifestyle or just help make ends meet a bit smoother. I had been telling people I was going to write this book since my last month of incarceration. And I had good intentions, but once you're free and blessed to be in different situations you kind of forget about promises you've made not only to others but to yourself. I have a few people that love me and that will do almost anything for me but still you must be able to do for yourself.

Reading about people you may idolize will help you visualize your plans. Make your dreams more relatable by seeing what obstacles hindered others and what they did to overcome. If it all failed today the only person, you'd have is yourself anyway, so you might as well be prepared. No one is going to see your vision but you. No one is going to make your dreams come true but you. Now, you may have a helping hand along the way but know that it is not guaranteed and don't take it for granted that it may exist. That is where faith in yourself will be a determining factor. You must be confident in your hand as if life is a card game and the hand that you have right now you are playing it until a new one is dealt. And as you play the game soon you may have the chance to become the dealer. But then never forgetting when the game seemed unfair to you. Self-determination is an important concept that refers to each person's ability to make choices and manage their own life. This ability plays an important role in mental health and a person's overall well-being. Self-determination allows you to tap into your inner self, and the ability to have control over their choices and lives. It should lead to some sort of motivation. Positive motivation moves mountains and makes barriers physical or mental seem like mole hills.

The lack of a support system doesn't mean failure. It guarantees a harder fight. And mental toughness will be a virtue and whenever success comes around, you'll have less people you may feel you owe any of it to. The best way to get even with those that you may feel didn't support you or have your back when needed is to succeed. Which is hard work.

Everyone can not help you become successful for numerous reasons. Some genuinely do not know what to do or how to do it or even if there are resources available to help your journey. Others may not have your best interest at heart. You have to train your mind to see the good in every situation. This is extremely hard but has to be done in order not to fall victim to life's ills. We all know people that won't get it together or can't get it together. Well in order not to be that person you have to train your mind the body and soul will follow.

EDUCATION

Well education is one of the most commonly overlooked essentials in life. While I was in the process of obtaining my associates degree, I learned that the only way to remove yourself from the social class you were born into is to amass an education or a great deal of wealth. Now a great deal of wealth is money that can't be messed up and you're back in the poor house tomorrow. The education will allow you to get more than a job a career will take you to the next tax bracket but without furthering your education and knowing what to do with new income will land you in debt. A high school diploma isn't enough to make it in this world. I believe a minimal requirement is an associate degree. Now obtaining this degree doesn't guarantee employment. But you're a hustler so the diploma is something to distinguish you from the guy next to you that wants the same job. If you really want to make yourself standout study for your master's degree. The degree that is earned is a tool to get a chance. This chance is not to be wasted but to be taken advantage of and conquered. The hard work and dedication it will take to excel in school will be the same once you make it to the boardroom. Nothing in this world will be accomplished without great sacrifice.

When applying that to the realm of education you must look at your end goal and figure out each step in between you and that goal. Each step in the educational process prepares an individual for what they will face in the next semester of classes and life. For example, while studying for my associates I had to work on cars to pay my bills. That was humbling and taxing on my body. I did incorporate some of the customer service lessons learned into my everyday life. This helped me to visualize a better day where I wouldn't smell like car exhaust and old oil. I progressed to entry level management while studying to obtain a bachelor's degree. In some areas this has helped me to obtain a few decent jobs that maybe could have materialized into a career. The ability to learn should be expounded on in every sense of the word. I don't believe the importance of education is pressed on the younger generation as much as other frivolous things. Also, everything learned may be repeated and seem useless, learn it. I have experienced this firsthand. In a class I may glaze over a concept and that very thing whether it be a vocabulary term or mathematical solution would be seen again at a later date. Then I'd have to learn something old just to add to it in hopes of grasping whatever knowledge in time to test well on the matter. That didn't play out too well. So, after that I made sure that I put maximum effort into my studies personally. Now that was always easy nor did it guarantee an A, but it did make sure that I passed with an above average grade and that I was prepared for the next phase of my education. I have done some reading while furthering my education. I have found that not enough emphasis is placed on secondary and post-secondary education. Especially in most of the middle-class environments and the story gets worse for those below the poverty line. The best solution to all of the above problems is a positive spin on education. I was always a smart guy but unfortunately being smart wasn't always the cool thing to be. And yes, unfortunately most people will put more effort into being "cool" than into becoming "successful". Isn't that mind blowing? We must curve the stereotype that gives children and young adults the impression that being uneducated is the thing to do.

MENTAL HEALTH

I decided to give mental health its own section. In the neighborhoods and sections I grew up in the only mental awareness I had was that some individuals received a check for being crazy they would say. The fact that many traumatizing situations have been witnessed while being on the porch and far worse things once off it. I had been told for the longest that I may need to seek counseling. I never took it serious until my thoughts began to not be as bright as they once were. Suicide is a touchy subject so I will just say this any problem that seems as it is too much or dwells on your conscious for too long seek counsel. One thing we can do ourselves to improve our mental health is exercise. By exercising the brain is able to process past events and or future ones as well. Also, endorphins are released which are known as the feel-good hormone which also fights stress. It's a win -win situation.

Make use of any mental screenings and or counseling available to you. I myself have begun seeing a counselor for overall betterment. Presently I attend college, so I make use of the services available there. It just so happens that my counselor told me to begin writing my thoughts down. I believe it was over Thanksgiving break. Emotions can scar a person for years then suddenly make their way to the surface. When that happened for me, I didn't have a support system to turn to but as I stated earlier, I was able to enlist the services at my University. If you're unable to get to a counselor right away here are a few things I have learned from my own personal struggles. Value yourself being proud of what you have accomplished thus far is a big start. At times we as a people get upset because we don't have what we want or the latest and greatest in whatever which distracts you from your goals.

Having a positive image of yourself gives you the will to succeed. To focus on one thing at a time will provide clarity on the subject or task at hand. Try not to multitask too much unless imperative and prioritize as much as possible this will keep the mind from wandering. If your mind starts to wander stop what you're doing and get back on task, however if you feel tired or drained it may be time to find a stopping point for today. I cannot emphasize this enough to exercise. Exercising has been such a powerful tool to improving my own mental health. And if you're a procrastinator it would help to try to begin your routine sooner in the day than later. Good meals make you feel good about yourself. Eating a home cooked meal or something prepared in an amazing way calms the soul. It makes you feel glad to be eating the dish and appreciative of life at the moment. Sleeping is sometimes overlooked. Lack of sleep leads to a bad mood and is a terrible for your mental health. I try to get at least eight hours of sleep. And if possible, try to rest at any period of the day just to breathe and self-evaluate. Self-evaluation for me is a time where I access what's going on presently how I feel about it and what I can do about it now and in the future. Your mind has to be strong enough to handle the mental aspect of your trials and tribulations just as much as your body has to be able to handle the physical activity associated with your endeavors.

THE BOARDROOM

The boardroom is unlike any place on earth. Any work establishment can and is your boardroom. And this space is filled with every characteristic of people you can imagine. Remember the heartless and ruthless acts seen on the block will not be present in corporate America but the same cutthroat mentality exists. And rightfully so it will be your job to obtain as must knowledge from these individuals with the least conflict. There will be plenty obstacles on your journey to the boardroom. Take mental note of any lessons learned good or bad because they may repeat themselves. The boardroom is a different hustle from block movements. But the mentality is the same it just must be applied differently. For example, you may have a job that starts at eight am but due to circumstances you may need to catch the bus at six am just to get there on time. The average person may feel that those tasks alone are too much and quit before they can even get started.

The same mindset it took to accomplish whatever one may want success in in the negative environment, use that grit, the determination, that me against the world attitude to accomplish something worth wild that won't cost your freedom. The trick to thriving in this and any environment like it is to have a thirst to succeed. To have a will to learn and to do so constantly and as much as necessary to remain an asset will be a daily task. Your first boardroom may not be a boardroom it may be frying chicken somewhere or flipping burgers whatever works. Life of course doesn't stop there and anything short of a career is just a steppingstone and should be looked at as such. Patience, Rome wasn't built in a day, but it was destroyed in one. So that's kind of something I say to myself to keep from making hasty decisions. It works sometimes and sometimes it doesn't. Also, my mother told me as a child that patience was a virtue, and that may be true. It's not a strength of many and in this microwave society we as people want whatever as fast like pronto. Like I stated earlier you'll run into all types of personalities in the workplace and many of them won't be pleasant. There are several ways to overcome this.

In every workplace, you will have difficult coworkers. Dealing with difficult coworkers, bosses, customers, clients, and friends is a skill worth perfecting. Dealing with difficult situations at work is stressful and will require every ounce of goodness you may possess. I have failed at this process every time. And that's ok because I was told long ago that I need to work for myself. I marginalize that to some capacity because of the economy we have and or certain responsibilities.

Difficult people are found in every single workplace. Difficult people come in every variety that you can imagine. But how difficult a person is for you to deal with depends a lot on your self-esteem, your self-confidence, how closely you must work with them on a daily basis. As

I stated before you will need to develop some type of poker face. That was one of the hardest things for me to do in the world. Coming from a place where your facial expressions usually show what's on your mind and how you're feeling at the time. You can ruin your job by not having the correct type of relationships with your coworkers at work. Your education, experience, or title don't matter if you can't play well with your coworkers. You won't succeed in your career without forming positive relationships at work. I had to add that because it is quite hard for me to deal with the different types of personalities that exist in the workplace. I have found myself to be nonconfrontational at work and I've even told a coworker I'm not going to argue with you because I was raised as a man if I need to raise my voice than there's a bigger problem and we should just go outside and fight like gentleman. That attitude has cost me a few jobs and I currently am trying to get rid of it from my everyday life.

I can recall working for a local automotive parts distributor as an assistant manager. Every day was a learning experience and I performed well as far as my numbers were concerned. However, when my manager transferred, I just knew I was going to receive his position. Wrong!! And to add insult to injury the person that filled that position was under qualified to numerous standards and was later fired for theft. Some of those things I and others had suspected but I didn't stick around to find out.

I've had managers that were so lazy that I ended up doing their job while they talked on the phone and ate lunch well ate from the time, they clocked in until the time they clocked out. Sometimes my academic background harmed my ability to keep gainful employment. And that meant to me that others had some type feelings to me trying to better myself in hopes of living a more comfortable life. Yeah, I parted ways with those type situations as well. Not always having a job lined up was a big mistake early on in my career. I have learned from those experiences not to do that anymore.

ENDING

I think the key to being successful at almost any transition is your willingness to except what is and your ability to progress to what you want it to be. I still have not yet reached my ideal boardroom. Every day I wake up I continue to try and put a plan together that will lead me to the promise land so to speak. The main point is to keep evolving until you become the person that you have envisioned for yourself. There is light at the end of the tunnel. You just must remember that your tunnel may be longer than expected. Personally, one thing that has always motivated me to do better for myself and my kids is the way I was raised as well as the events I feel have shaped my life so to speak. The impossible is very possible depending on how much time and effort you want to put into them. And let me tell you that the results you see are in direct correlation to those efforts. One thing that helps to motivate me daily is a new day. Like how people look at a new year I try to visualize a better day be offered when I open my eyes. Because truthfully a lot of people don't wake up once they've fell asleep. The act of waking up is the first of many blessings you may receive in a day. I hope that no one looks at this and thinks I have it all figured out because I don't. I just revert to the tools I have pick up along the way to do the best job I possibly can. While hallway through this project I was faced with an obstacle that left me with two thoughts. Quit or Keep it going. I choose to keep it going. That decision took a few hours to come to the light. I was even late to an interview. Nothing comes in life without sacrifice. Even when situations aren't the greatest and the outcome seems uncertain keep fighting.

Diplomacy as far as I am concerned is the professional activity of managing internal relations. Now these internal relations can be any emotion, any topic, and any reason that prevent constructive living. I say constructive because it is work like the construction business. And to build a building you start with the bottom. And then my friend you level up. After that you repeat the process of building the leveling up you have to continue until you reach you desired accomplishments. And once you do that hopefully you apply those principles to all aspects in life and strive for perfection. To improve is to evolve but, perfection is to evolve constantly. So, in that constant effort of becoming better a good habit is formed a passion is created and these things will help you when times are tough. When you're the first and last line of defense all you can count on will be yourself. I hope that after reading this you feel better equipped to tackle some things in your own personal life.

CPSIA information can be obtained
at www.ICGtesting.com
Printed in the USA
LVHW090324141120
671369LV00007B/693

9 781646 203505